Portugal

by Kari Schuetz

BLASTOFF! READERS 5

BELLWETHER MEDIA · MINNEAPOLIS, MN

Note to Librarians, Teachers, and Parents:

Blastoff! Readers are carefully developed by literacy experts and combine standards-based content with developmentally appropriate text.

Level 1 provides the most support through repetition of high-frequency words, light text, predictable sentence patterns, and strong visual support.

Level 2 offers early readers a bit more challenge through varied simple sentences, increased text load, and less repetition of high-frequency words.

Level 3 advances early-fluent readers toward fluency through increased text and concept load, less reliance on visuals, longer sentences, and more literary language.

Level 4 builds reading stamina by providing more text per page, increased use of punctuation, greater variation in sentence patterns, and increasingly challenging vocabulary.

Level 5 encourages children to move from "learning to read" to "reading to learn" by providing even more text, varied writing styles, and less familiar topics.

Whichever book is right for your reader, Blastoff! Readers are the perfect books to build confidence and encourage a love of reading that will last a lifetime!

This edition first published in 2012 by Bellwether Media, Inc.

No part of this publication may be reproduced in whole or in part without written permission of the publisher. For information regarding permission, write to Bellwether Media, Inc., Attention: Permissions Department, 5357 Penn Avenue South, Minneapolis, MN 55419.

Library of Congress Cataloging-in-Publication Data

Schuetz, Kari.
  Portugal / by Kari Schuetz.
     p. cm. – (Blastoff! readers : exploring countries)
  Includes bibliographical references and index.
  Summary: "Developed by literacy experts for students in grades three through seven, this book introduces young readers to the geography and culture of Portugal"–Provided by publisher.
  ISBN 978-1-60014-733-3 (hardcover : alk. paper)
  1. Portugal–Juvenile literature. I. Title.
  DP518.S38 2012
  946.9–dc23   2011034269

Printed in the United States of America, North Mankato, MN.
010112   1203

Contents

Where Is Portugal?   4

The Land   6

The Azores   8

Wildlife   10

The People   12

Daily Life   14

Going to School   16

Working   18

Playing   20

Food   22

Holidays   24

Age of Discovery   26

Fast Facts   28

Glossary   30

To Learn More   31

Index   32

**Atlantic
Ocean**

Portugal

Spain

⭐ Lisbon

Did you know?

According to Greek legend, the warrior Odysseus founded Lisbon while on his long journey home from Troy.

**Gulf of
Cádiz**

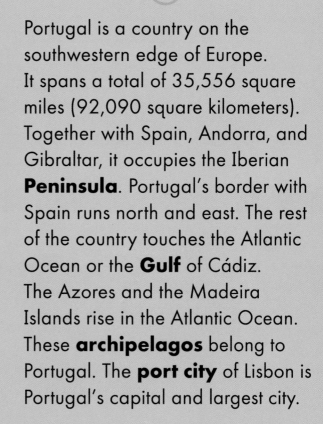

Portugal is a country on the southwestern edge of Europe. It spans a total of 35,556 square miles (92,090 square kilometers). Together with Spain, Andorra, and Gibraltar, it occupies the Iberian **Peninsula**. Portugal's border with Spain runs north and east. The rest of the country touches the Atlantic Ocean or the **Gulf** of Cádiz. The Azores and the Madeira Islands rise in the Atlantic Ocean. These **archipelagos** belong to Portugal. The **port city** of Lisbon is Portugal's capital and largest city.

The Tagus River divides Portugal into northern and southern halves. This major river begins in Spain and empties into the Atlantic Ocean. Mountainous terrain and high **plateaus** dominate northern Portugal. The Estrela Mountains, or Star Mountains, are known as "the roof of Portugal." They rise in the north to heights over 6,500 feet (1,980 meters).

Rolling hills and plains fill most of southern Portugal. South of the Tagus River, cork oaks and olive trees grow in the Alentejo region. **Limestone** caves and **grottoes** stretch along the coastline of the Algarve region below, which is known for its beautiful beaches.

Tagus River

Atlantic Ocean

Azores

Portugal

Mount Pico

N

W   E

S

Portuguese explorers first discovered the Azores in the early 1400s. The Azores are the tops of mountain peaks rising out of the middle of the Atlantic Ocean. Nine islands make up this Portuguese archipelago. They include Pico Island, which has Mount Pico, Portugal's highest point.

The Azores formed from **volcanic eruptions** on the sea floor. The islands lie where three **tectonic plates** meet. Today, earthquakes and volcanic eruptions can disrupt life for the islanders of the Azores.

Did you know?
Some people believe that the Azores are remains of Atlantis. This is the lost civilization that the Greek philosopher Plato wrote about hundreds of years before the Azores were discovered.

Mediterranean monk seal

Did you know?
The endangered Mediterranean monk seal hides in underwater caves off the coast of Portugal.

Iberian wolf

fun fact

The Egyptian mongoose attacks venomous snakes in Portugal's forests. The mongoose is immune to the poison of the deadly snakes!

Egyptian mongoose

Portugal's landscape supports a variety of rare animals. The Spanish ibex roams Portugal's mountain forests. This wild goat is found only in Portugal and Spain. The **endangered** Iberian wolf also lives only on the Iberian Peninsula. Deer, rabbits, wild pigs, and the ibex must watch out for this predator.

European bee-eater

Other animals are much more common in Portugal. In the limestone-rich south, European chameleons flick their tongues at rapid speed to catch moths and other insects. The coast is a stop for many **migrating** birds. European bee-eaters, griffon vultures, and storks use Portugal as a place to rest. Dolphins, whales, sardines, and other fish swim in the coastal waters.

Did you know?

Native Portuguese descend from many different people groups. Their ancestors include Iberians, Celts, Romans, Moors, Jews, and Germanic tribes.

Portugal is home to almost 11 million people. Nine out of every ten people are **native** Portuguese. Brazilians, Chinese, and those from Portugal's past Asian and African **colonies** make up most of the remaining population. Small groups of Marranos and Roma also live in Portugal. Marranos are **descendants** of Jews, and the Roma are descendants of people who came to Europe from India hundreds of years ago. Portuguese, the official language of Portugal, is spoken by most of the population. People in a small area of northeastern Portugal also speak Mirandese.

Speak Portuguese!

English	Portuguese	How to say it
hello	ola	oh-LAH
good-bye	boa-tarde	BOH-uh-tard
yes	sim	seeng
no	não	nowng
please	faz favor	FAWSH fuh-VOR
thank you	obrigado	oh-bree-GAH-doh
friend (male)	amigo	ah-MEE-goh
friend (female)	amiga	ah-MEE-gah

trolley

Over half of Portugal's population lives in cities along the Atlantic coast. One out of every three people lives in Lisbon or Porto. In Lisbon, old traditions blend with new ones. Fish vendors called *varinas* wander the streets with baskets of fish on their heads. Ship horns blare from the ports as people ride **trolleys** through the city streets.

14

People in the countryside live on farms where they gather their own food. They have festivals that last several days and are often in honor of a **patron saint**. The walls of many churches and other buildings across the country are covered with *azulejos*. These are beautiful polished ceramic tiles covered in blue and white artwork.

Where People Live in Portugal

countryside
39%

cities
61%

fun fact
Portugal's cobblestone streets are works of art. The stones form designs of waves, ships, and sea monsters.

Children in Portugal usually go to school from ages 6 to 15. These nine years of basic education are split into three stages. Stage one includes grades 1 through 4. Students in these grades learn Portuguese, math, and art. The second stage is grades 5 and 6. History and music are introduced at this level. Grades 7 through 9 make up stage three and have classes covering foreign languages and sciences. Students receive a certificate at the end of the third stage.

Once students have earned this certificate, they can choose to attend three years of secondary school. During these years, students can focus on general subjects or **vocational** courses. Students who finish secondary school can attend universities or technical schools.

Where People Work in Portugal

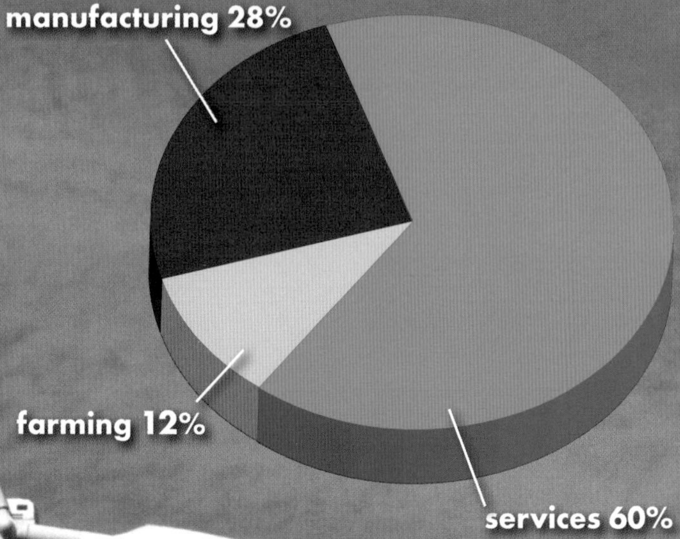

manufacturing 28%

farming 12%

services 60%

Did you know?

Portugal is a leader in alternative energy. The country uses the sun, the sea, and the wind as major sources of power.

Many Portuguese hold **service jobs** to assist the country's **citizens** and **tourists**. People work in places such as stores, restaurants, and banks. Fishers bring in catches of sardines, tuna, and cod for both visitors and locals to enjoy. In factories, workers make cement, auto parts, and clothing. They also make cork and paper from Portugal's trees.

Land in the countryside is used for farming and mining. Important crops include grains, potatoes, grapes, olives, and tomatoes. Farmers also raise sheep, cattle, and pigs. Miners dig into the earth for tungsten, tin, chromium, and copper. These **minerals** are sent to factories where they are made into products.

! fun fact

In Lisbon, people clap after listening to *fados*. People in Coimbra cough to applaud the songs.

Folk music is a big part of Portuguese culture. People often visit cafés in the evening to listen to folk songs called *fados*. They also enjoy many traditional dances, including the *vira* and *fandango*. The *vira* is similar to the waltz, a three-beat ballroom dance. In the *fandango*, two dancers take turns showing off their steps. The *terreiro*, or dance floor, is a main gathering place in almost every town.

The bullring is another place that draws crowds. People come to watch bullfights. In Portuguese bullfights, the *matador* is on horseback. Portuguese follow the sport of soccer even more closely. Some businesses close so their employees can watch the national team play! The Portuguese also enjoy sailing, surfing, and scuba diving off the Atlantic coast.

bacalhau

Fish and other seafood fill most plates in Portugal. Meals are usually served with vegetables and fruits. The national dish is *bacalhau*, which is salted codfish. The Portuguese use hundreds of different recipes to prepare this dish.

When fish is not on the menu, the Portuguese enjoy soups and pork dishes. *Caldo verde* is a popular soup made with potatoes, onions, cabbage, and sometimes sausage. People often eat strong cheeses made from sheep or goat milk before or after a main dish. Desserts flavored with cinnamon are commonly served at the end of a meal.

caldo verde

pastel de nata

fun fact

In the 1700s, Catholic nuns created many traditional Portuguese pastries. One sweet they made is *pastel de nata*, a cinnamon-flavored custard tart.

The Portuguese celebrate many religious holidays. These include Christmas, Easter, and All Saints' Day. Children visit their neighbors to collect cakes and nuts on All Saints' Day. It is also tradition for families to bring flowers to the graves of dead relatives. *Carnaval* is another major holiday in Portugal. People celebrate by wearing large, colorful masks and decorating floats for lively parades.

Portugal's most celebrated national holidays are Liberty Day, Portugal Day, and Republic Day. All of these days celebrate Portugal's independence. Portugal Day, on June 10, is also called Camões Day. It honors Luís Vaz de Camões, a Portuguese poet famous for writing about the country's journeys of discovery.

Did you know?

Portuguese explorers had to be brave. Many people believed that the uncharted waters were full of sea monsters and whirlpools.

San Gabriel,
Vasco da Gama's ship

Bartolomeu Dias

Vasco da Gama

! **fun fact**

In 1488, Portuguese explorer Bartolomeu Dias became the first European to sail around the southern tip of Africa.

In the 1400s, Prince Henry the Navigator turned Portugal into a **hub** of ocean exploration. He built a center where Portuguese explorers studied **navigation** and developed the caravel. This style of ship had sails that made it faster and easier to direct than other ships.

Portugal focused on finding new routes for sea travel around the world. Bartolomeu Dias, Vasco da Gama, and others sailed to Asia, where they could trade for spices and other goods. Portuguese explorers also set sail to gain more territory. The colonies they established influenced the culture of Portugal and made it a world power.

Portugal's Flag

More than half of Portugal's flag is red. This represents the blood shed by those who have defended the country. The rest of the flag is green and represents hope. Portugal's coat of arms sits where the red and green colors meet. It is a symbol of the voyages and settlements of early Portuguese explorers. The flag was officially adopted in June of 1911.

Official Name: Portuguese Republic

Area: 35,556 square miles (92,090 square kilometers); Portugal is the 111th largest country in the world.

Capital City:	Lisbon
Important Cities:	Porto, Amadora, Braga, Setúbal
Population:	10,760,305 (July 2011)
Official Languages:	Portuguese, Mirandese
National Holiday:	Portugal Day (Camões Day) (June 10)
Religions:	Christian (86.7 %), Unknown (9%), None (4%), Other (0.3%)
Major Industries:	farming, fishing, forestry, manufacturing, services, technology, tourism
Natural Resources:	cork, iron ore, copper, zinc, tin, tungsten, silver, gold, uranium, marble, clay, gypsum, salt, timber, fish
Manufactured Products:	textiles, paper products, rubber, chemicals, auto parts, plastics, ceramics, glassware, machinery, ships
Farm Products:	grains, potatoes, tomatoes, olives, grapes, sheep, cattle, goats, pigs, poultry, dairy products
Unit of Money:	euro; the euro is divided into 100 cents.

Glossary

archipelagos—groups of islands

citizens—people who enjoy the national rights of the country in which they live

colonies—territories controlled and settled by people from another country

descendants—younger family members who are all related to one older family member

endangered—at risk of becoming extinct

grottoes—small caves

gulf—a part of the ocean extending into land

hub—a center of activity

limestone—hard stone that forms over millions of years from old coral and shells

migrating—moving from one place to another, often with the seasons

minerals—elements found in nature; tungsten and copper are examples of minerals.

native—originally from a specific place

navigation—the science of finding one's way in unfamiliar territory

patron saint—a saint who is believed to look after a country or group of people

peninsula—a section of land that extends out from a larger piece of land and is almost completely surrounded by water

plateaus—areas of flat, raised land

port city—a city located by a sea harbor where ships can dock

service jobs—jobs that perform tasks for people or businesses

tectonic plates—sections of Earth's crust that can move, causing earthquakes and volcanic eruptions

tourists—people who are visiting a country

trolleys—streetcars powered by overhead electrical wires

vocational—related to specific jobs

volcanic eruptions—explosions of lava, steam, and ash; over time, volcanic eruptions can form mountains.

To Learn More

AT THE LIBRARY

Deckker, Zilah. *Portugal*. Washington, D.C.:
National Geographic, 2009.

Koestler-Grack, Rachel A. *Vasco da Gama and
the Sea Route to India*. Philadelphia, Pa.: Chelsea
House Publishers, 2006.

Mis, Melody S. *How to Draw Portugal's Sights and
Symbols*. New York, N.Y.: PowerKids Press, 2005.

ON THE WEB

Learning more about Portugal
is as easy as 1, 2, 3.

1. Go to www.factsurfer.com.

2. Enter "Portugal" into the search box.

3. Click the "Surf" button and you will see a list of
   related Web sites.

With factsurfer.com, finding more information is just
a click away.

Index

activities, 20, 21
Age of Discovery, 24, 26-27
All Saints' Day, 24
Azores, 5, 8-9
Bartolomeu Dias, 27
capital (see Lisbon)
Carnaval, 24
colonies, 13, 27
daily life, 14-15
earthquakes, 9
education, 16-17
explorers, 26, 27
food, 22-23
holidays, 24-25
Iberian Peninsula, 5, 10
landscape, 6-9, 10
languages, 13, 16
Liberty Day, 24
Lisbon, 4, 5, 14, 20
location, 4-5, 8
Mount Pico, 8
peoples, 12-13
Porto, 14
Portugal Day (Camões Day),
    24
Prince Henry the Navigator,
    27
Republic Day, 24
sports, 21
Tagus River, 6

transportation, 14
Vasco da Gama, 26, 27
volcanoes, 9
wildlife, 10-11
working, 18-19